Grow a Giant Beanstalk

And **15** more amazing plant projects!

by Sandra Markle
Illustrated by Eric Brace

SCHOLASTIC INC.

New York Toronto London Auckland Sydney
Mexico City New Delhi Hong Kong Buenos Aires

For Lynn Walker for helping to make my home garden beautiful.
—S.M.

For Lumpy and Bumbles,
the best pet fish a guy could ask for.
—E.B.

The author would like to thank Dr. Tony Conner, Soil Plant and Ecology Sciences, Lincoln University, Lincoln, New Zealand, for sharing his expertise and enthusiasm. As always, a special thanks to Skip Jeffery for his help and support.

No part of this publication may be reproduced in whole or in part, or stored in a retrieval system, or transmitted in any form or by any means, electronic, mechanical, photocopying, recording, or otherwise, without written permission of the publisher. For information regarding permission, write to Scholastic Inc., Attention: Permissions Department, 557 Broadway, New York, NY 10012.

ISBN 0-439-44434-9

Text copyright © 2003 by Sandra Markle.
Illustrations copyright © 2003 by Scholastic Inc.
All rights reserved. Published by Scholastic Inc.
SCHOLASTIC and associated logos are trademarks and/or registered trademarks of Scholastic Inc.

12 11 10 9 8 7 6 5 4 3 2 1   3 4 5 6 7 8/0
Printed in the U.S.A.   40
First printing, April 2003
Design by Jennifer Rinaldi Windau

SCIENCE DARES YOU TO...

Get green!	5
Grow a giant beanstalk	9
Make a plant escape a box	11
Make a heart appear on a leaf	16
Put more pop in popcorn	21
Make seeds open a bottle	26
Make a jack-o'-lantern disappear	31
Give celery stalks red stripes	35
Make plants water themselves	39
Make roots grow up instead of down	44
Grow plants without soil	48
Sprout garbage	53
Grow a clone	56
Dare yourself!	63

Note to Parents and Teachers: The books in the Science Dares You! series encourage children to wonder why and to investigate to find out. While they have fun exploring, young readers discover basic science concepts related to each book's theme. They also develop problem-solving strategies they can use when tackling any challenge.

In *Science Dares You! Grow a Giant Beanstalk*, children tackle challenges that help them become empowered to ask questions and seek solutions. In the process, they develop an understanding of green plants by investigating their physical structure, what they need to grow, and how they reproduce. "Organisms have basic needs. For example, plants require air, water, nutrients, and light. Organisms can survive only in environments in which their needs can be met. Plants and animals have life cycles that are different for different organisms." (National Science Education Standards as identified by the National Academy of Sciences.)

SCIENCE DARES YOU TO **GET GREEN!**

What if you could grow a **GIANT** beanstalk, make seeds pop the top off a plastic bottle, or build a mini-world where plants never have to be watered? Believe it or not, you can do all these things—*and lots more*—when you tackle the dares in this book. All you need is your creativity, a little help from Science, and some amazing **living things**:

GREEN PLANTS.

The Basics

First, you need to know something about green plants. Unlike people and animals, green plants are able to produce food within their bodies. This process is called *photosynthesis*. To make food, green plants use a special green coloring matter—*chlorophyll*—to trap light energy. This light energy converts water and carbon dioxide gas from the air into sugars. Oxygen, a gas people and animals need to breathe, is released into the air as a waste gas.

Green plants have a system of tubes, called *xylem* tubes, to transport water up to where food is being produced—usually in the leaves. Other tubes, called *phloem* tubes, transport the food down to the stem and roots to be stored. Food moves downward mainly by gravity. But water moves upward through the plant because of evaporation, water moving into the air, from the leaves. This creates a suction force on the water within the plant, pulling the water up through the xylem tubes.

Like animals, green plants reproduce. Usually the result is a special cell, called a seed. When seeds have water, minerals, and a suitable temperature, they sprout. Then the young green plants start growing and producing food. And the life cycle begins all over again.

be careful

STAY SAFE!

Always check with an adult partner to be sure the way you plan to meet each dare will be safe for you to try.

Never, ever put anything you are testing into your mouth unless you know it's safe to do so.

You're almost ready to get green and put plant power to work for you. But first, here are some tips that will help you meet each science challenge.

HELPFUL HINTS

 Brainstorm ways to tackle the challenge. Use the clues provided to help you think of possibilities. Then list three to five things you could try.

 Choose which ideas would be most likely to work. Don't forget to check with an adult to be sure your idea is safe for you to test.

 Test your idea. Then read over the suggested way to meet the challenge. Try it, too. Then decide if this approach provides some ideas you might use to modify and improve your solution.

Now you're ready to get green. Good luck—and don't forget to have fun!

GROW A GIANT BEANSTALK

Your challenge is to make bean plants grow super tall in just a week without using fertilizer. You can do it—with a little help from science.

Clues

✗ Soak a bean seed overnight and then carefully pry it open along the groove. You'll see the tiny plant inside and two *cotyledons*. The cotyledons hold stored food. How could this help you meet the dare?

✗ Bean plants, like other green plants, need sunlight to produce their own food. Could this help you meet the dare?

TAKE THE DARE!

You'll need:

- **10 dried soup beans**
- **Bowl**
- **Water**
- **Sharp pencil**
- **2 Styrofoam cups**
- **Potting soil**
- **Clear wrap**
- **2 sturdy paper plates**

1. Select seeds that are whole and have an unbroken seed coat.

2. Put the seeds in the bowl, cover them with water, and soak overnight.

3. With your pencil, poke three holes in the bottom of each cup.

4. Fill the cups nearly full with potting soil.

5. The next day, plant five seeds in each cup.

6. Sprinkle the soil with water and cover with clear wrap.

7. Set one cup on a plate in a warm, sunny spot. Place the other cup on a plate inside a dark cupboard.

8. Check every day, and when the seeds sprout, remove the clear wrap. Add water as needed to keep the soil damp. Within a week, you'll have grown giant beanstalks. But you may be surprised to discover that the tallest plants are the ones that grew in the dark.

What Happened?

Plants need sunlight to produce food energy. So plants grown in the dark use up their stored food, growing taller in search of sunlight.

MAKE A PLANT ESCAPE A BOX

Your job is to find a way to make bean plants grow so their stems bend toward a hole in a box. But no touching the plants to shape their stems!

Clues

- ✗ Have you ever noticed a houseplant whose leaves are all aimed in one direction—toward a window? Why might this have happened?

- ✗ Gently bend a beanstalk plant. You will discover that the stem is strong but flexible. How can this trait help you meet the dare?

TAKE THE DARE!

You'll need:

Scissors
Box with a lid or flaps
A pot containing three to five newly sprouted bean plants
  (If possible, use a variety of runner beans.)
Towel

1. Use the scissors to poke a hole the size of a quarter in one side of the box, about two inches (five centimeters) from the top.

2. Make the hole larger until it's about as big around as the bottom of a juice glass.

3. Open the box and place the pot of bean plants inside.

4. Move the beans as far away from the hole as possible.

5. Cover the box with the towel to keep any light from seeping inside from any spot other than the hole. Only open the box to water the plant.

6. Position the box so the hole is aimed toward a window. The amount of time this dare will take depends on how fast the beans grow. But within a few days, the plants should be longer and bent toward the hole. As they grow, they should push their stems out of the hole, proving you've succeeded.

What Happened?

Were you surprised to discover the plant moved? Green plants need sunlight. If possible, they will grow in a way that lets their leaves absorb as much of the sun's energy as possible. The bean plant moved by making one side of the stem—the part away from the light—grow faster than the other. That caused the plant to bend and grow toward the light.

Plants growing in shady places will bend and twist in order to expose their leaves and flowers to sunlight. In fact, some plants change their position every day to be sure leaves or flowers receive just the right amount of sunlight. Sunflowers move their big flower head around to follow the sun throughout the day. So do wood-anemones and hawkweed. But exposure to full sun can damage some leaves. That's why eucalyptus trees in Australia turn their leaves edgeways to the sun, protecting them from being scorched. The compass plant that grows on sunny North American prairies also twists its leaves to protect them from the burning midday blast of sunlight.

WOW! It probably wouldn't even take a day for a kudzu vine to grow out of the box. Kudzu grows as much as 12 inches (30 centimeters) a day during warm summer months. No wonder this vine sometimes kills whole forests by growing over the trees!

Another fast grower is bamboo. Although it can grow up to 164 feet (50 meters) tall and look like a tree, bamboo is really a superfast-growing grass. Some types of bamboo grow up to 3 feet (about 1 meter) per day and can be as much as 60 feet (18 meters) tall in less than three months.

One other superfast-growing plant is a kind of seaweed called **Caulerpa taxifolia**. This plant doesn't just get taller. It multiplies, producing lots more seaweed in record time. And as it grows, the seaweed spreads over the sea bottom, choking out the other plants fish need to eat. In one area in France, divers have been trying to pull up **Caulerpa**, stopping its spread. So far, the seaweed is still winning.

DOUBLE DARE #1

Science dares you to make a sweet potato escape a box.

MAKE A HEART APPEAR ON A LEAF

Don't worry. You won't need magic to meet this dare. You just need to understand how green plants make food—the clues will help you figure it out.

Clues

- Green plants need sunlight to produce *chlorophyll*, the green substance they need to produce food. Prove this to yourself by sprouting three bean plants in a dark closet. They'll be white or pale yellow. How could this need for sunlight help you meet this dare?

- If it's summertime and the grass is green and growing, set a large rock or a piece of wood on the grass. Leave it for three days. When you remove the object, you'll see that the grass underneath is now yellow because it stopped being exposed to sunlight. How could what happened help you meet the dare?

TAKE THE DARE!

You'll need:

Construction paper
Scissors
2 large paper clips
Potted geranium

1. Cut out a two-inch (five-centimeter) square from the construction paper.

2. Fold the paper in half and snip half a heart along the centerfold.

3. Unfold the paper heart.

4. Carefully clip it onto one of the geranium's largest leaves.

5. Set the plant where it will be exposed to full sunlight.

6. After a week, carefully remove the paper heart to discover a pale heart shape on the leaf. Congratulations, you've met the dare!

What Happened?

When you blocked sunlight to part of the leaf, chlorophyll production stopped in that part of the leaf. Then, the covered part of the leaf changed color. You just got a peek at what other coloring pigments the leaf contained. Most leaves contain yellow or orange pigments in addition to green chlorophyll. But the green coloring masks these other hues.

When leaves appear to change color in the fall, these other pigments are being unmasked, just the way they were in the geranium's leaf. As the hours of daylight decrease, many trees stop the food-making process in their leaves. Then the production of chlorophyll needed for this job stops, too. As the chlorophyll breaks down, the green disappears and the other colors are revealed. At the same time, other chemical changes may occur, producing even more colors. For example, a red pigment can form from any sugars trapped in the leaves. This makes some leaves look fiery red.

A Historic Dare

How do you supply plants with the light they need to grow on a space station or a colony on Mars? Scientists are meeting this dare by using Light Emitting Diodes, or LEDs. These lights let scientists give plants only the type of light they need to grow. Did you know that plants need red and blue light, not green light, to grow?

WOW! The plants with the largest leaves are the raffia palm and the Amazonian bamboo. Some of these leaves grow as long as 65 feet (about 20 meters).

DOUBLE DARE #2

Science dares you to design an experiment to test whether exposing bean plants to 24 hours of continuous sunlight makes them grow taller.

PUT MORE POP IN POPCORN

Have you ever noticed that not every popcorn kernel pops when you make popcorn? Your challenge is to find a way to get fewer duds.

Clues

- ✗ Examine a handful of popcorn kernels. Each one has a tiny wood-colored tip. While you can't see it, there's a little hole in this tip. How might this fact help you meet the dare?

- ✗ What happens when popcorn pops? Inside each kernel, there is a soft blob of something called starch. This contains water. When popcorn gets hot enough, the water turns into steam. That breaks open the kernel's tough seed coat, and the soft starch expands into a fluffy mass. The kernel needs the water to pop, so how can you make sure it contains water?

TAKE THE DARE!

You'll need:

- **Measuring cup**
- **Popcorn kernels**
- **Hot air popcorn popper**
- **Bowl**
- **Measuring spoons**
- **Water**
- **Plastic storage container with a lid**

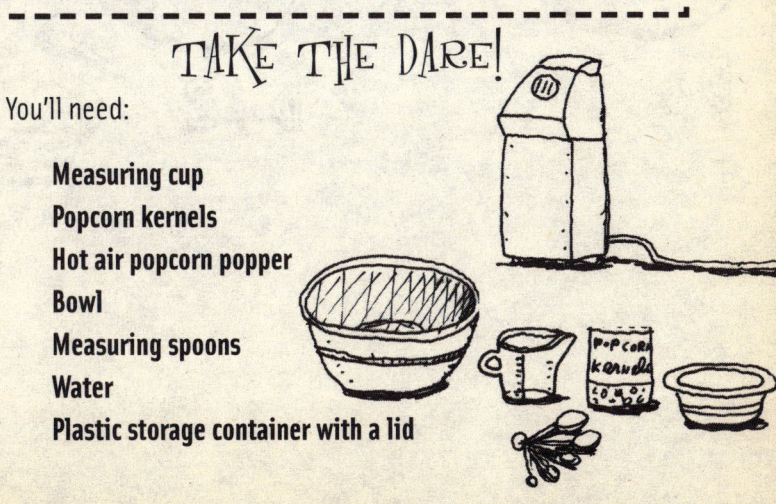

1. Pop one cup of popcorn and count the number of duds in the bottom of the bowl.

2. Pour a second cup of the same popcorn into the container, add one tablespoon of water, put on the lid, and shake a few times.

3. Let the popcorn sit in the sealed container overnight.

4. Pop the corn. You should see fewer duds, proving you've met the dare. If you still get as many duds as before, repeat the process. This time, add a tablespoon of water each day for two days before popping.

What Happened?

The tiny hole in a popcorn kernel lets water out as well as in. So sometimes popcorn kernels dry out. Without water to turn into steam, these kernels won't explode. Tossing the popcorn with water lets any dry kernels soak up needed moisture. That way, more of the kernels contain enough water to pop.

WOW!
- Popcorn is an ancient snack. Popcorn kernels have been found in Incan tombs estimated to be more than a thousand years old. Even older ears of popcorn were found in Bat Cave in New Mexico. These were estimated to be more than five thousand years old. But that early popcorn wouldn't have produced much of a snack. Each ear was only about two inches (five centimeters) long. And each individual popcorn kernel was enclosed in its own husk.

A Historic Dare

From ancient times, popcorn lovers had to tackle the challenge of how to pop up the corn. One early way was to stab an oiled ear of corn with a stick and hold the ear near a fire. But soon inventive popcorn lovers developed the first poppers. These were carved from soapstone or molded from pottery and metal. Some of the earliest poppers have been discovered at the sites of ancient Indian dwellings. It's believed these containers had lids and were set directly in the flames. Later, corn was popped in a cylinder of thin sheet iron that could be cranked to make it spin around in front of the fire. These were often used to pop corn for breakfast. Popcorn was served with sugar and cream as the first "puffed" cereal. During the Depression years (1929-1939), big steam- or gas-powered poppers were invented. These allowed vendors to move from place to place, selling popcorn to people on the street. In the 1950s, popcorn was packaged in special aluminum containers that could go right on the stove. Then these poppers also became the popcorn serving dishes. Today, modified versions of these make it possible to pop corn in the microwave.

MAKE SEEDS OPEN A BOTTLE

How could you make bean seeds change so they get bigger? That's what you'll need to do to make seeds pop the top off a plastic film canister.

Clues

- Compare the size of a dry sponge to one that's been soaked in water. The wet one will look bigger. How could water help you meet this dare?

- Remember what you discovered about how popcorn kernels can take in water. How might this help you change the bean seeds?

TAKE THE DARE!

You'll need:

Plastic film canister with snap-on lid
Dried soup beans
Water

  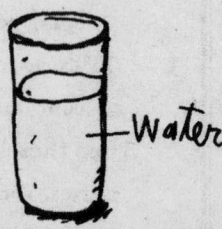

1. Fill the film canister to the top with bean seeds.

2. Slowly add water until the canister won't hold any more.

3. Snap on the lid and let the canister sit overnight.

4. In the morning, check the canister. You'll discover the lid has been pushed up, proving you've met the dare.

What Happened?

Look closely at a soup bean. If possible, use a magnifying glass. You'll see what looks like a dividing line, and near one end of this is a hole. The water entered the seeds. As the stored food material inside each seed got wet, it swelled up. And each bean got bigger around. Because the film canister was full to start with, the swollen beans pushed off the lid.

WOW! The seeds of giant sequoia trees actually get started with the help of forest fires. Giant sequoias produce their seeds in egg-sized cones. Heat from a forest fire dries these cones. Then they open and each releases as many as 500,000 tiny seeds. Meanwhile, the fire turns logs and dead branches on the forest floor to ash. This creates a fertile bed where the young sprouts can start to grow.

DOUBLE DARE #3

Science dares you to design an experiment to test whether seeds soaked in water overnight sprout faster than dry seeds.

A Historic Dare

THERE WERE ONCE HUNDREDS OF CALVARIA trees on the island of Mauritius in the Indian Ocean. By the 1970s, only 13 remained. Scientists wanted to find a way to save this tree from extinction, but nothing they tried would make the seeds sprout. Then a scientist named Stanley Temple figured out why new trees weren't sprouting. All of the living trees were about 300 years old. Their seeds had stopped sprouting about the time a bird called the dodo became extinct. Temple figured the dodo ate the tree's fruit. The seed's coat was too tough for the plant to sprout by itself. But when the bird's gizzard ground up the fruit, it weakened the seed's coat just enough to let it sprout. So to meet this dare, Temple fed the calvaria tree's fruit to turkeys. Many of the seeds were softened enough to sprout by the time they were passed with the turkeys' droppings.

MAKE A JACK-O'-LANTERN DISAPPEAR

You have to meet this dare without touching the jack-o'-lantern. Sound impossible? Don't worry. You can do it with a little help from science.

Clues

- Every autumn, many trees drop their leaves. So why aren't the forests full to the treetops with dead leaves? Bacteria and fungi make the leaves rot away. How might fungi and bacteria help you meet the dare?

- Put a slice of white bread on a plate and sprinkle it with water. Set the plate inside a warm cupboard. Within a few days, the bread will have fuzzy fungi growing on it. This fungi came from the air. How might the fact that there is fungi in the air help you meet this dare?

TAKE THE DARE!

You'll need:

- Newspapers
- Adult partner
- Safety knife
- Pumpkin
- Spoon

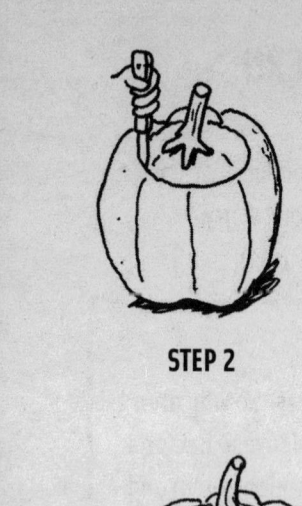

STEP 2

STEP 3

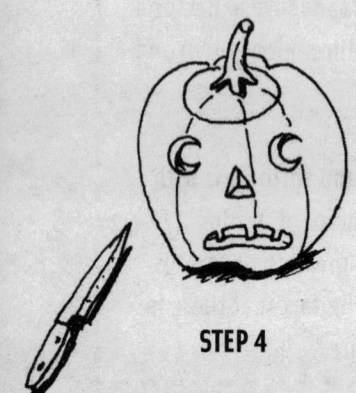

STEP 4

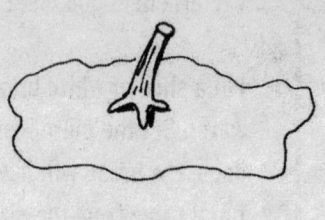

STEP 5

1. Work outdoors or indoors on newspapers.

2. Have your adult partner help you cut a lid in the pumpkin.

3. Scoop out the seeds and carve a face.

4. Set the jack-o'-lantern outdoors, on the ground. Check with your adult partner about where you should put the jack-o'-lantern, because it will produce liquid as it rots.

5. Be patient. Depending on the weather, it will take as long as two to three weeks for the pumpkin to rot. But once it does, you've met the dare.

What Happened?

Fungi are plants, but they usually aren't green. This is because they don't make their own food. They get the food energy they need by using an animal or another plant for food. In this dare, fungi in the air settled on the pumpkin. Next, the fungi spread threadlike strands through the jack-o'-lantern. Even tinier bacteria gave off special juices that broke down whatever they touched. This changed the pumpkin's tissue into a liquid food for the fungi and bacteria. Eventually, only the tough outer skin and stem of the pumpkin remained. The rest of it disappeared.

WOW! In Australia, the brush turkey's nest is a lot of rot! In fact, when researchers weighed one big nest, they discovered it contained 14,994 pounds (6,800 kilograms) of rotting plants. Rotting plant material generates heat. So instead of sitting on their eggs to incubate them, brush turkeys bury their eggs and let the rotting plants keep the developing chicks warm.

DOUBLE WOW! Would you believe that rotting plants can also preserve human bodies? That's what happened in peat bogs. Peat is made up of partially rotted plants plus bits of dead insects, yeast, and fungi. The plant material prevents oxygen from reaching the water that seeps down and builds up in the bog. Acids given off by all of the rotting material build up, too. So conditions in the bog are just right for human tissues to be preserved. Mummylike bodies of people have been recovered from bogs in Europe. One, called the Tollund Man, was found in a bog in Denmark in 1950. He was wearing a leather hat and, although his skin looked like tanned leather, his features were still clearly visible. Scientists estimated the man's body was about 2,000 years old.

GIVE CELERY STALKS RED STRIPES

Can you make red stripes appear on a stalk of celery without using any paint? Check out the clues for ideas.

Clues

- Take a drink through a straw. This is how a green plant gets water. Special tubes carry water from the soil up from the roots, through the stem, to the leaves. How can these tubes help you meet the dare?

- Check with an adult partner to be sure you have permission to perform this test. Then put a plastic bag over the leaves of a healthy houseplant and carefully tie it around the plant's stem. Set the plant in a sunny spot. Check in a couple of hours, and you'll see droplets of moisture inside the bag. This water passed out of the plant through tiny holes in the leaves. Could this fact help you meet the dare?

TAKE THE DARE!

You'll need:

- Water glass
- Water
- Red food coloring
- Scissors
- Celery stalk with leaves

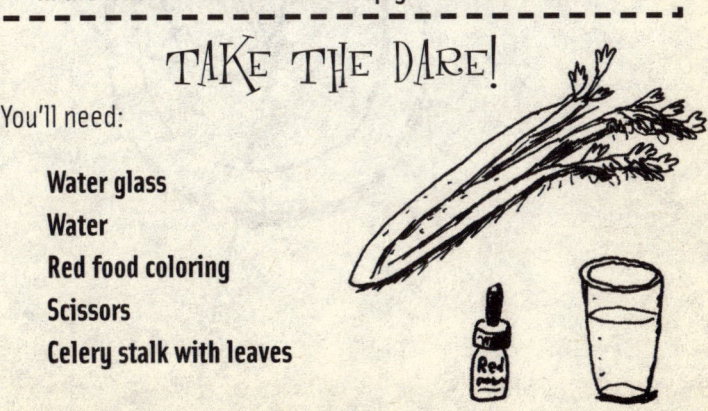

1. Fill the glass about two-thirds full with water and add three drops of red food coloring.

2. Snip just a little off the larger end of the celery stalk. This should be the end without leaves.

3. Place the cut end into the water and let the stalk sit overnight.

4. In the morning, use the scissors to cut lengthwise through the celery stalk. You'll see red stripes, showing that you successfully met the dare.

What Happened?

Like other plants, celery has a circulation system of tubes, called *xylem* and *phloem*, to transport water and food. Xylem tubes carry water from the roots up to the stems and leaves. Phloem tubes carry food down from the leaves to the rest of the plant. In this case, colored water passing through the xylem tubes stained them red. That made the tubes appear to be red stripes in the celery stalk.

A plant's phloem tubes remain alive while its xylem dies after a year. So the plant develops new xylem tissue every year. During the spring, the xylem tubes that form are made up of large cells. Then during the summer, the xylem tubes that form are made up of smaller cells. This difference in tube size from spring to summer creates growth rings: light spring rings sandwiched between darker summer rings. So counting either light rings or darker rings in a dead tree can tell you how many years a tree lived. A tree's xylem tissue also shows what the growing seasons were like. Trees produce wide growth rings in wet years and narrow growth rings in dry years. Scientists study very old trees to learn what the weather was like in Earth's ancient past.

WOW! To reach the top of a giant redwood called the Mendocino Tree, water has to rise 368 feet (112 meters). That California tree is the tallest tree anyone has discovered so far. And the Mendocino Tree is still growing!

DOUBLE WOW! By counting tree growth rings, scientists have discovered that some trees have lived for more than 4,000 years. The bristlecone pines that are native to the Rocky Mountains of the United States are believed to be around 4,600 years old—probably the oldest living organisms on Earth.

MAKE PLANTS WATER THEMSELVES

Meet this dare, and you'll have found a way to make plants recycle water.

Clues

✗ A damp cloth dries when water evaporates or moves into the air. How could you keep the water in the cloth from evaporating?

✗ If you put a plant inside a plastic bag, water droplets will eventually appear inside the bag. How could this help you meet this dare?

TAKE THE DARE!

You'll need:

- Adult partner
- Scissors
- Clear plastic gallon-size (or two- to three-liter) juice bottle with a screw-on plastic cap
- Gravel
- Potting soil
- Small houseplants (Choose plants that require the same conditions, including full sun or shade.)
- Water
- Electrician's tape or duct tape

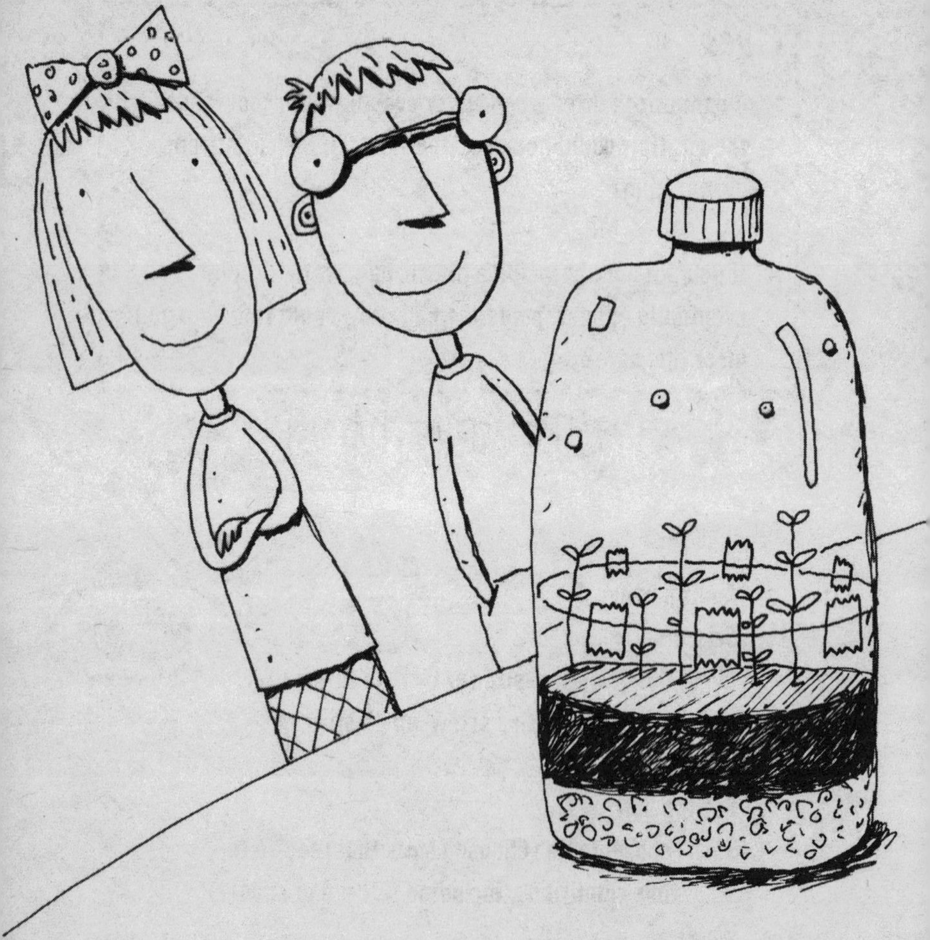

1. Have your adult partner cut the top off the bottle about a third of the way up from the bottom.

2. Pour enough gravel into the bottle's base to cover the bottom.

3. Fill the base about half full with potting soil.

4. Dig the plants into the soil.

5. Sprinkle on water until the soil is damp.

6. Set the top on the base and anchor it with tape. Use more tape to seal the top to the bottom.

7. Screw on the bottle cap.

8. Set it where it will get the amount of sunlight the plants require. When you see water droplets rain down the inside of the bottle walls, you've met the dare. The plants are watering themselves. You've just created something called a terrarium.

What Happened?

Water evaporated from the moist soil. But the plants also gave off water through their leaves. The lower side of each leaf has lots of tiny holes. These let air in and out. During photosynthesis, plant leaves use the carbon dioxide in the air to produce food. And they give off oxygen as a waste gas that escapes through the leaves' holes. But water also escapes out through these holes in the plant's leaves. In fact, a full-sized tree is likely to lose as much as 80 gallons (363 liters) of water in a day. That's not wasting water, though.

Plants don't have hearts to pump water up from the roots to the leaves. But water evaporating from the leaves causes fresh water to be drawn into the roots and up through the stem or trunk. This water carries along minerals from the soil that the leaves need to produce food. Only about one percent of all of the water a plant draws in through its roots is actually used by the plant during photosynthesis. The rest is given off through the leaves to keep water circulating.

Inside the terrarium, the water vapor released into the air was trapped. The moist air rose until it came in contact with the cooler walls of the bottle. Cooling caused the water in the air to condense or change back into water droplets. Then the droplets dripped back to the soil and soaked in. There the water could be drawn in again by the plant's roots, repeating the process.

A Historic Dare

IN 1827, DR. NATHANIEL WARD was frustrated that his ferns were being killed by smoke from London's factories. Then he discovered a healthy fern growing in a little soil inside a glass jar. Deciding that the only way to save his plants was to give them their own miniworld, he built a miniature greenhouse. These miniworlds, called terrariums, became so popular that by the 1860s nearly every home had one.

WOW! Cornwall, England, is home to the Eden Project, or biomes under glass. The Humid Tropics biome is the world's largest miniworld, stretching 787 feet (240 meters) long, 360 feet (110 meters) wide, and 164 feet (50 meters) high. This man-made rainforest contains more than 1,000 different kinds of plants. These have been grown from seeds and cuttings supplied by nurseries around the world. Some of these are plants in danger of becoming extinct in the wild. So the Eden Project has given them a new, safe place to grow. The climate inside this glass-covered world is computer controlled to be just right for a rainforest. Overhead sprayers and waterfalls keep the air moist. And an extensive ground irrigation system provides all the water the plants need without soaking visitors.

MAKE ROOTS GROW UP INSTEAD OF DOWN

If you jump up, a force called gravity pulls you back to Earth's surface. Does this same force affect the direction roots grow? Or can you plant a seed so its sprouting roots grow toward the sky?

Clues

✗ Roots take in the plant's supply of water. How could you use water to encourage roots to grow up instead of down?

✗ Soak dried lima beans or other bean seeds overnight in water. Carefully split apart the two halves of the seeds to find the tiny plant inside. You'll see that one end has leaves and the other end has a root. How would turning the seeds in different directions affect the direction the roots grow?

TAKE THE DARE!

You'll need:

Dried bean seeds, such as soup beans
3 clear plastic cups
Water
3 paper towels
Newspaper
Clear plastic wrap

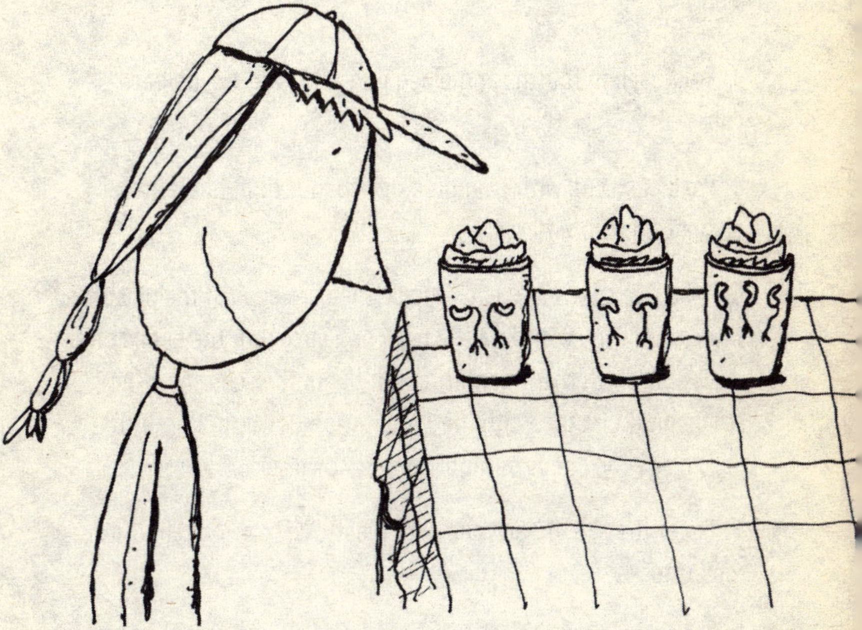

1. To speed up the sprouting process, place at least 20 bean seeds in a cup, cover with water, and soak overnight.

2. The next day, pick out 15 unbroken seeds to plant.

3. Wet the three paper towels and squeeze out the excess water.

4. Fold each in fourths and place one as a liner inside each cup.

5. Pack each cup with crumpled newspaper to hold the towel against the cup wall.

6. Poke five seeds into each cup so they are against the plastic, where you can easily see them. In one cup, turn the seeds on their side, with the indentation up. In another cup, turn the seeds on their side, with the indentation down. In the third cup, place the seeds straight up and down.

7. Cover the top of each cup with plastic wrap to hold in the moisture.

8. Set the cups in a warm location. Within a day or two, the seeds should sprout. Once the roots grow for a day or two, you should see them all turn down. Luckily for the plants, this is a dare you can't meet!

(A)   (B)   (C)

What Happened?

No matter what position the seeds were planted, the roots grew downward. That was in response to Earth's gravity. Once they get started, roots will grow outward as well as downward, searching for water. At the tip of each root, there is a tough cap that protects the root as it pushes through the hard grains of soil. Just behind this cap, the root cells multiply, making the root grow longer and pushing the root tip through the soil. Some root tips secrete an oily substance that helps the root burrow more easily. The growing section of the root is also covered with tiny root hairs. These absorb water from the soil and help hold on to the soil grains, anchoring the plant.

WOW!
- Not every plant has its own roots. A process called grafting allows the stem of one plant to be permanently attached to the roots of another plant. Grafting is done to help less strong plants survive. For example, the stems of some delicate kinds of roses are grafted on to strong wild rose roots.

GROW PLANTS WITHOUT SOIL

You see plants growing in the ground outside in the yard, in the park, and even in flowerpots. But did you know plants are able to grow without soil? If you can figure out how, you'll meet this dare.

Clues

✗ Think about what green plants need to grow: minerals, water, air, and sunlight. Minerals and water are supplied by the soil. Where else could they come from?

✗ Look for information about duckweed and elodea. These plants get the minerals they need from something other than soil. What is it?

TAKE THE DARE!

You'll need:

- Scissors
- Styrofoam cup
- Plastic tub with a snap-on lid (such as a margarine tub)
- 1" x 10" (2.5 cm x 25 cm) strip of an old T-shirt
- Water
- Liquid fertilizer
- Cotton balls
- 3 bean seeds
- Bowl

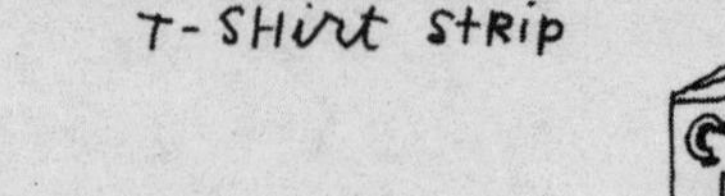

Plant Presoaked seeds

Cotton Balls

T-shirt strip

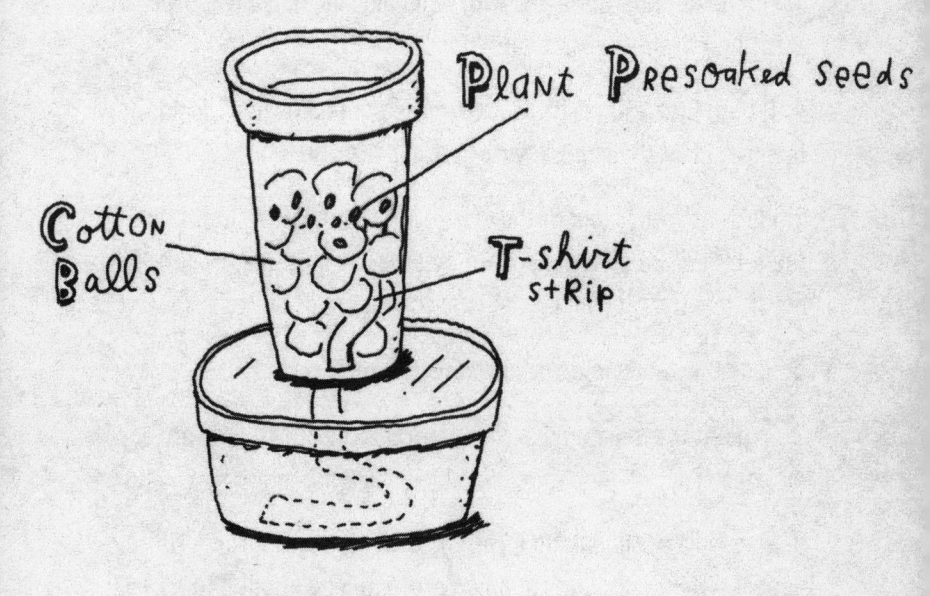

Tub Filled 2/3 with water and 1/3 Liquid fertilizer

1. Cut a slot in the bottom of the cup and in the tub's lid.

2. Make the slots just big enough for the T-shirt strip to slide through easily.

3. Fill the tub two-thirds full with water and add liquid fertilizer according to the package directions.

4. Thread the T-shirt strip a little more than halfway up inside the cup. Stuff the cup full with cotton balls.

5. Place the other end of the cloth strip through the slot in the tub's lid. Be sure the strip submerges as you snap the lid on the plastic tub. The cup will now be on top of the tub.

6. Soak the seeds in a bowl of water overnight.

7. To plant the seeds, poke them into the cotton. Cover with more cotton.

8. Place in a warm, sunny location. In a few days, sprouts will appear. When the plants keep on growing long enough to produce leaves, you've met this dare.

What Happened?

This method of growing plants is called *hydroponics*. In your experiment, the minerals were supplied by the water and not by soil. The cotton balls supported the plants and let both nutrient-rich water and air reach the plants' roots.

A Historic Dare

AFTER A WAR WITH their neighbors, the ancient Aztecs were driven from their homeland onto the marshy shore of Lake Tenochtitlán in Central America. Their dare was to find a way to grow crops so they could survive. Because there was no good soil on the shore, they built floating reed rafts and covered them with soil dredged up from the lake bottom. On these, they grew vegetables, flowers, and even trees, whose roots grew down into the water. The Aztecs turned the swampy lake into a floating garden.

TWO WEEKS LATER

SPROUT GARBAGE

SCIENCE DARES YOU!

Are beet tops, avocado pits, and half a shriveled potato just garbage, or could these plant parts have a second life? Your dare is to get at least one of these to sprout.

Clues

- Find the "eyes," or indentations, on a potato. Look for what appears to be a white bump in one of these eyes. Does it look like a tree bud? It should, because it *is* a bud. The potato has several of these buds. How could this help you meet the dare?

- Have you ever noticed green shoots sprouting from carrots that have been in the refrigerator for more than two weeks? The carrot is actually the plant's root. The shoots are using the food energy stored in the root to grow. Could other vegetables produce sprouts, too?

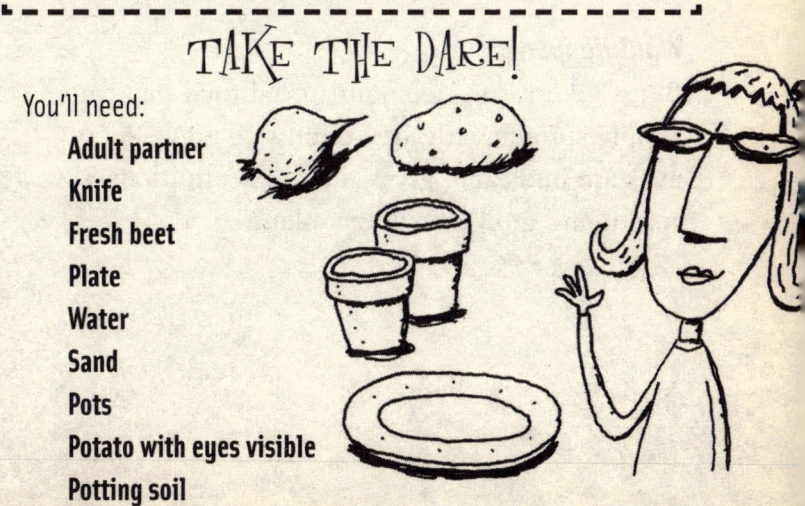

TAKE THE DARE!

You'll need:
- **Adult partner**
- **Knife**
- **Fresh beet**
- **Plate**
- **Water**
- **Sand**
- **Pots**
- **Potato with eyes visible**
- **Potting soil**

1. Have your adult partner cut off the top of a beet at its fatter end, leaving about one inch (2.5 centimeters) of the plant.

2. Place the beet, cut surface down, on a plate of water. Or plant the beet top in sand so that just the top is exposed.

3. Keep water on the plate, or keep the sand moist. Leaves will appear in about two weeks.

4. Place the whole potato or a part of it containing at least one eye in a container of potting soil, so the potato is completely covered.

5. Put the container in a warm but not sunny place and keep the soil moist.

6. Sprouts will appear in one to two weeks.

What Happened?

Beets, like carrots, contain stored food that can supply sprouts with food energy to grow. Potato eyes are buds and, given suitable conditions, can sprout and grow into a new plant.

WOW! One 200-acre forest of aspen trees in Utah is really a grove of plant clones. Scientists studying tissue samples from the trees in this forest discovered each tree sprouted from one parent tree's roots. While cloning is natural for aspens, this forest is the largest ever discovered.

DOUBLE DARE #4

`Science dares you to force bushes, like pussy willow and forsythia, to bloom early.`

DOUBLE WOW! According to the Guinness Book of World Records, the biggest potato ever grown weighed just over seven pounds (about three kilograms). In 1990, the Pringle's Company in Jackson, Tennessee, produced the world's largest potato chip. It measured 23 inches by 14.5 inches (57 centimeters by 36 centimeters). But that chip wasn't a single slice from one superbig spud. It was produced from processed potatoes.

GROW A CLONE

Your challenge is to grow a plant that is a clone, meaning it's identical in every way to the parent. Plants have been doing it to themselves for years.

Clues

- Spider plants produce what look like little plants on the ends of long stems. If one of these little plants grew into a new plant, would it be exactly like the bigger plant?

- Gardeners sometimes take cuttings from plants and use these to grow new plants. Could this help you meet the dare?

TAKE THE DARE!

You'll need:

- Sharp pencil
- 2 Styrofoam cups
- Potting soil
- Geranium plant
- Sturdy plastic plate
- Water

Step 1

Step 2

Step 3

Step 4

Step 5

Step 6

Step 7

1. Use the pencil to poke three drainage holes in the bottom of the two cups.

2. Fill the cups with potting soil.

3. Find one small branch on one of the geranium's main stems. Be sure it has at least two leaves. Break it off carefully right where it joins the bigger branch.

4. Push the broken end of the stem into the potting soil.

5. Set the cup on the plate in a warm, sunny spot. Water daily just enough to keep the soil moist.

6. In about a week, you'll see new leaves appear.

7. When the new geranium gets bigger, it will produce leaves and flowers that are identical to the parent plant. And you will have met the dare.

What Happened?

The new plant you grew came from a piece of the parent plant. So its tissues and its appearance are identical to the parent plant. Gardeners often use cloning to produce plants they can count on to have specific desirable features.

Amazing Green Plants!

WOULD YOU BELIEVE a sunflower isn't really one flower? It's a cluster of more than two thousand tiny flowers growing together.

A RARE HERB called *Puya raimondii* grows to be about 150 years old before it ever flowers. Once the blooms are finished, the plant dies.

WATER HEMLOCK AND spotted hemlock produce two of the deadliest poisons in the world. But they're kin to two vegetables that are good for you: carrots and celery.

ACACIAS PROTECT THEMSELVES from animals that eat them by having large thorns. But some animals, like giraffes, have long tongues to pull leaves from between the thorns. So acacias also have bulblike hollows at the base of each thorn, providing a place for army ants to live. When an animal tries to tear off leaves, the ants rush out and bite, defending their home and saving the plant's leaves.

DOUBLE DARE SOLUTIONS

#1 A sweet potato will escape the box by producing a vine that grows out through the hole. To plant the sweet potato, pick one small enough to fit easily into a drinking glass that will fit inside the box. Stick four sturdy wooden toothpicks into the sweet potato near its rounder end. Set the potato on the glass and fill the glass half full with water. Add water every few days as needed. If the sweet potato doesn't sprout within a week, start growing it on a sunny windowsill and then transfer it to the box.

#2 First, predict whether you think bean plants exposed to 24 hours of sunlight each day will grow taller in two weeks than ones that receive only six hours of exposure. To test this, you'll need a grow lamp and six identical bean plants that have the same size pot and identical soil and receive the same amount of water sprinkled on the surface each day. Be careful to expose the one group of plants to the grow lamp for just six hours at the same time each day. Measure all the plants at the beginning of the test, at the end of the first week, and again at the end of the second week. At the end of the test, also compare the condition of the two sets of plants. Being taller isn't always better—if the plant is spindly, it could break easily in a strong wind.

#3 You may have developed another design for your experiment, but here's one to try. First, count out 20 dried soup beans and soak 10 of them overnight. Then wet two identical paper towels, squeeze out the excess water, and slide each into a self-sealing plastic bag. Place the 10 soaked seeds on the towel in one bag. Place the 10 dry seeds on the towel in the other bag. Close both bags but don't seal them. Place the bags side by side in a warm place and check daily to see which sprouts first. Repeat the test two more times to be sure the results are likely to happen every time.

DOUBLE DARE SOLUTIONS

#4 Outdoors, have your adult partner help you find a pussy willow or a forsythia bush. Pick branches with tight buds. Have your adult partner cut the end of the branch at an angle. Then place the cut end on a piece of wood and have your adult partner hit it with the hammer, flattening it. Place the flattened end in a container of warm water and set in a warm, sunny place indoors.

You've provided the conditions the plant normally needs to bloom, and you've done it a little ahead of when those conditions would happen in nature. Most bushes will bloom only about a month earlier than usual.

DARE YOURSELF!

Congratulations! You've successfully met the dares presented in this book. You're not finished, though. Now science dares you to use what you've discovered about green plants: how seeds sprout, how plant growth is affected by sunlight and gravity, and how plants transport water from the roots to the leaves. Then brainstorm and plan experiments of your own. Check with an adult partner to be sure that what you want to try is safe to test. And let science help you meet all the dares you can dream up!

SCIENCE WORDS

CHLOROPHYLL The green pigment in plants that absorbs the sun's light energy and changes it into chemical energy. The plant uses the energy to produce sugar and a waste gas—oxygen.

CLONING Growing a new plant from a part of the parent plant, such as a stem.

CONDENSATION The process of water vapor (water in the air) changing to liquid water.

COTYLEDON Supplies stored food to sprouts in some kinds of plants. It is also called the seed leaf.

HYDROPONICS Growing plants in a liquid rather than in soil.

PHLOEM System of tubes in a plant through which food moves down to be stored in the stem and roots.

PHOTOSYNTHESIS The process of changing light energy to chemical energy using chlorophyll.

XYLEM System of tubes in a plant through which water and minerals move between roots and leaves.